STOP Blaming the Adversary: It's YOU!

MINISTER JEREMY B. SIMS

Sims Consulting

Contents

CHAPTER ONE

Introduction

Throughout history, humans have sought reasons for their misfortunes, mistakes, and challenges. Often, in religious contexts, it's been easy to point the finger at an external entity - the Adversary. But what if this blame is misplaced? What if the true root of our challenges lies within? In "Stop Blaming the Adversary: It's You," we explore the transformative power of self-realization, the importance of personal responsibility, and the spiritual growth that stems from acknowledging our choices. Dive in to chart a new path forward, grounded in accountability and the freedom that comes from truly owning your journey.

CHAPTER TWO

THE POWER OF THE TONGUE – THE MORE YOU BLAME AND CALL (the adversary) NAME

Have you ever paused to consider the weight and impact of your words? The ancient wisdom asserts that life and death lie in the power of the tongue. What you utter, the narratives you spin, and the names you invoke bear an energy that can influence, shape, and mold your experiences and perceptions.

Think back to a moment when someone's words uplifted you, causing your spirit to soar. Conversely, remember a time when a careless comment left a sting, echoing in your mind long after it was spoken. That's the potency your words hold. They can heal or hurt, create or destroy, uplift or tear down. Now, consider this: when you consistently attribute your challenges, mistakes, or misfortunes to external forces or beings, what reality are you weaving for yourself?

Invoking a name, especially that of the Adversary, is not merely an act of utterance. Every time you lay blame and call upon his name, you are, in essence, relinquishing a portion of your power and agency. You're subtly suggesting that you're at the mercy of external forces, rather than an active participant in shaping your destiny. It's an easy path, isn't it? To attribute your missteps or hardships to external entities. But in doing so, you unknowingly empower the very thing or being you blame.

Consider the narratives you've clung to. Have you ever caught yourself saying, "The devil made me do it," or attributing a lapse in judgment to outside temptations? While external influences are undoubtedly present, it's crucial to understand that every choice, action, or word spoken begins within. You have the autonomy to decide, respond, and act.

Imagine the transformation that awaits when you shift your focus from external blame to internal reflection. What if, instead of uttering words of blame, you speak affirmations of strength, resilience, and growth? The energy and reality these words create can be profoundly different. Your words can become a powerful tool for introspection, growth, and empowerment.

In your spiritual journey, remember this: the power of the tongue is immense. Every word you utter, every name you invoke, casts a stone into the waters of your existence, creating ripples that shape your reality. So, as you move forward, choose your words with intention and wisdom. Recognize the narratives you've been holding onto and ask yourself, "Do they serve or hinder my growth?" Your path, lit by the words you speak, is yours to chart. Choose words that empower, enlighten, and elevate. For in doing so, you reclaim the reins of your journey and stride forth with clarity and purpose.

***

***

CHAPTER THREE

The Adversary: Misunderstood and Misblamed

A deeper look at how blaming external entities, especially the Adversary, has historical roots and the implications of this misplaced blame.

The concept of the Adversary, in one form or another, has been a cornerstone in many religious and philosophical systems around the world. This entity, whether named Satan, Lucifer, Mara, or any other title across diverse cultures, often represents opposition, temptation, or even outright evil. Historically, this being has been the embodiment of everything that counters the will of the divine, a necessary counterpart to represent free will, choice, and the moral struggles inherent in human existence.

Historical texts, scriptures, and folklore from various civilizations and religions, be it Abrahamic or Eastern traditions, often depict a figure or force that tempts, opposes, or challenges the righteous path. But here lies the crux of the matter: the Adversary, while often portrayed as a tempter or deceiver, is rarely depicted as having direct control over human free will. It presents choices, challenges, perhaps even illusions, but the decision to act remains with the individual.

Over time, however, there has been a shift in perception. The Adversary, rather than being seen as a symbolic representation of the challenges we face in our moral and spiritual journeys, has become a convenient scapegoat for human failings. Instead of understanding the character as a narrative tool to explain the nature of temptation and the importance of free will, many have taken a more literal approach, attributing personal and societal shortcomings directly to this external entity.

This misinterpretation has profound implications. By externalizing blame and attributing our misdeeds or misfortunes to the Adversary, we create a barrier to self-awareness and personal growth. We deny ourselves the opportunity to reflect on our actions, to understand our motivations, and to grow from our experiences. Instead of acknowledging our flaws and working to overcome them, we absolve ourselves of responsibility.

This perspective also impacts communal growth. In societies where the Adversary is blamed for wide-scale problems or challenges, there's less motivation for collective introspection or societal reform. When the root of problems is attributed to an external supernatural force, it shifts the focus away from tangible solutions.

Furthermore, this misplaced blame has a tendency to dilute the richness and depth of religious teachings. When focus shifts from internal reflection and growth to external blame, the profound lessons of scriptures risk being overshadowed.

However, it's essential to recognize that the concept of the Adversary, when understood in its true symbolic context, holds valuable lessons. It serves as a constant reminder of the moral and spiritual challenges we face, the temptations that lurk, and the importance of free will and personal responsibility. But to unlock these lessons, we need to shift our perception and understand the Adversary not as an external force controlling our destiny but as a representation of the choices and challenges inherent in the human experience.

As we delve deeper into the journey of spiritual maturity, it becomes imperative to reframe our understanding of the Adversary. Only by doing so can we truly take charge of our actions, learn from our experiences, and embark on a genuine path of spiritual growth and enlightenment.

CHAPTER FOUR

Self-Reflection: The Starting Point of Change

I n the quiet corners of our minds, beyond the cacophony of daily life and the relentless barrage of external stimuli, there exists a space - a sanctuary where the soul can introspect. This space, often overlooked in the hustle and bustle of modern living, is the realm of self-reflection. It is here that the journey of true change commences, and it's from this point that spiritual growth sprouts.

Self-reflection, at its core, is the art of looking inward. Instead of casting our gaze outwards to external forces or circumstances, it is about turning that gaze inwards, examining our thoughts, emotions, actions, and motivations. It is an exploration of the self, seeking to understand who we are, why we act the way we do, and how we relate to the world around us.

But why is self-reflection so pivotal in our spiritual journey? Simply put, without awareness of our current state, we cannot hope to grow or evolve. Just as a gardener must first assess the condition of the soil before planting, we too must understand our inner landscape if we wish to cultivate a rich spiritual life.

Recognizing our flaws is an integral aspect of this introspective journey. All of us, no matter how advanced on our spiritual path, have imperfections. It might be pride, impatience, a tendency to judge, or countless other human frailties. By reflecting upon these, not with self-judgment but with a desire to understand, we can begin to address and transform them.

Furthermore, self-reflection helps us understand the decisions we've made and the paths we've chosen. Life is a series of choices, each one leading us down a particular road. By contemplating these choices, we gain clarity about our motivations and desires. Were they driven by ego? Fear? A genuine calling? By understanding our past decisions, we can make more enlightened choices in the future.

However, this process is not always comfortable. Peeling back the layers of our psyche can reveal truths that are difficult to face. But it's important to remember that this discomfort is a natural part of growth. Just as a seed must rupture its shell to sprout, we too must confront and move beyond our limitations to blossom spiritually.

Moreover, self-reflection is deeply intertwined with many religious teachings. Scriptures across various faiths emphasize the importance of inner examination. For instance, the Bible states, "Examine yourselves to see whether you are in the faith; test yourselves" (2 Corinthians 13:5). Such verses underscore the significance of introspection in one's spiritual journey.

In today's world, with distractions aplenty, setting aside time for self-reflection can seem challenging. Yet, it's crucial to prioritize this practice. Whether it's through meditation, prayer, journaling, or quiet contemplation, dedicating moments to introspection can be profoundly transformative.

As we progress in this book and explore the path of spiritual maturity, it's essential to keep returning to this sanctuary of self-reflection. For it is from this place of understanding, clarity, and awareness that we can truly embark on the profound journey of spiritual growth and transformation.

***

Assessment Tools:

1. Daily Reflection Journal

Instructions: Every night, spend 10-15 minutes writing about your day. Focus on emotions, reactions, and decisions. Where did you excel? Where could you have done better?

What it does for you: This tool helps capture patterns in behavior and thinking, allowing you to identify areas for growth and celebrate small victories.

2. Emotional Reaction Tracker

Instructions: Each time you have a strong emotional reaction (positive or negative), jot it down. Identify the trigger, the emotion, and how you responded.

What it does for you: Understanding your triggers can equip you to handle them better in the future.

3. Guided Self-Reflection Questionnaires

Instructions: Once a week, fill out a questionnaire that prompts deeper introspection. Questions might include: "What did I learn about myself this week?" or "When did I feel most aligned with my values?" *What it does for you:* These structured queries guide you in diving deeper into your self-awareness journey.

4. Visual Mood Board

Instructions: Create a board with images, quotes, or items that resonate with your current emotions or state of mind. Update it as your feelings evolve.

What it does for you: A visual representation can sometimes capture nuances of feelings that words cannot.

5. Mind Mapping:

Instructions: Start with a central idea or feeling in the center of a page. Draw branches that represent related thoughts, feelings, or actions. Explore how they interconnect.

What it does for you: Mind maps help you visually understand the complexities and layers of your thoughts, giving clarity to otherwise abstract concepts.

6. The "Three Whys" Technique:

Instructions: For any strong emotion or reaction, ask yourself "Why do I feel this way?" to the response, ask "Why?" again, and once more after that.

What it does for you: This method digs deep into the underlying reasons behind your feelings, helping to unveil core issues or beliefs.

7. Meditation and Mindfulness Apps:

Instructions: Use apps that guide you in mindfulness exercises, focusing on the present moment without judgment.

What it does for you: Regular mindfulness practice can enhance self-awareness, helping you become more attuned to your inner self.

8. Feedback Sessions:

Instructions: Periodically, ask close friends or family for feedback on certain behaviors or patterns they've observed in you. Approach it with an open mind.

What it does for you: Sometimes, an external perspective can highlight areas for reflection you hadn't previously considered.

Engaging in self-reflection is akin to looking into a mirror, not just to see the surface but to understand the depths beneath. By using these tools consistently, you're taking proactive steps toward positive change, fostering growth from the inside out. Remember, it's a continuous journey, and every insight, no matter how small, is a step forward.

CHAPTER FIVE

Accountability: Taking Charge of Our Choices

A DISCUSSION ON HOW TAKING RESPONSIBILITY EMPOWERS INDIVIDUALS TO STEER THEIR LIFE AND SPIRITUAL JOURNEY.

Every choice we make, every action we take, carries with it a consequence. As the ripples spread out across the pond of existence, they shape our reality and mold our future. The key to navigating these waters of life lies in a simple yet profound concept: accountability. By taking charge of our choices, acknowledging their consequences, and understanding the role we play in creating our reality, we set forth on a path of empowerment and spiritual enlightenment.

Accountability is a cornerstone of personal growth and spiritual evolution. It signifies a deep understanding that our actions, words, and thoughts are not isolated events but are interconnected pieces of a larger tapestry. But what does it mean to truly be accountable?

Being accountable means taking ownership of our actions, both good and bad. It's acknowledging when we've made a mistake, without shifting the blame to external factors or individuals. It's recognizing our role in a particular situation or outcome and understanding that our choices have led us to this point.

This isn't to say that external circumstances don't play a role in our lives. They do. But accountability is about recognizing that even amidst external influences, we always have a choice in how we respond. The true power lies not in the situation itself but in our reaction to it.

By embracing accountability, we empower ourselves. No longer are we passive spectators in the theater of life, but we become the directors, capable of steering the narrative. This shift from a reactive to a proactive stance is transformative. When we understand that we hold the reins of our destiny, we can guide our spiritual journey with purpose and intention.

Moreover, from a spiritual perspective, accountability draws us closer to the Divine. Many religious texts emphasize the importance of personal responsibility. For instance, Galatians 6:5 (KJV) states, "For every man shall bear his own burden." This reinforces the idea that individual responsibility is not just a societal expectation but a divine mandate.

Additionally, accountability fosters a deep sense of humility. By acknowledging our imperfections, we cultivate a mindset of continuous learning and growth. This humility opens the doors to grace, forgiveness, and spiritual progress.

However, it's crucial to differentiate between accountability and self-blame. While the former is empowering, the latter can be destructive. Taking responsibility shouldn't be an exercise in self-flagellation but a step towards understanding and growth.

In our journey of spiritual maturity, accountability serves as a compass. It guides us through the maze of choices, illuminates the path of righteousness, and helps us navigate the challenges that life presents. By taking charge of our choices, by understanding their implications, and by continuously striving to align our actions with our spiritual goals, we not only enrich our lives but also contribute positively to the world around us.

In the chapters that follow, as we delve deeper into the facets of spiritual growth, let the principle of accountability be our guiding light, reminding us of the power we possess and the potential we have to shape our spiritual destiny.

***

Assessment Tools:

1. Choice Mapping:

Instructions: Whenever you're faced with a decision, map out the potential outcomes of each choice. This will help you visualize the consequences and rewards of your actions.

What it does for you: Helps you make more informed decisions by projecting possible outcomes.

2. Decision Diary:

Instructions: Keep a diary where you document each significant decision you make, the reasons behind it, and the outcome.

What it does for you: Over time, this will highlight patterns in your decision-making and provide insights on where you might be acting impulsively or wisely.

3. Values Clarification Exercise:

Instructions: List down your core values. Whenever faced with a choice, check if it aligns with these values.

What it does for you: Ensures that your choices resonate with your inner beliefs and principles, leading to more fulfillment.

4. Pros and Cons List

Instructions: The age-old method of jotting down the advantages and disadvantages of any significant choice.

What it does for you: A simple way to weigh your options and see what the best course of action might be.

5. Accountability Partner

Instructions: Pair up with someone you trust. Whenever you're about to make a big decision, discuss it with them.

What it does for you: Offers an external perspective and someone to ensure you follow through with your decisions.

6. Pause and Reflect Technique

Instructions: Before making any decision, especially impulsive ones, take a deep breath, count to ten, and then decide.

What it does for you: Helps curb impulsive decisions, giving your brain a moment to process and choose wisely.

7. Outcome Visualization

Instructions: Visualize the potential long-term outcomes of your choices. How will they affect you in a day, a month, a year?

What it does for you: Encourages foresight and the consideration of long-term consequences.

8. Feedback Analysis

Instructions: After decisions, ask for feedback from those affected. Understand how your choices impact others.

What it does for you: Promotes empathy in decision-making and can highlight areas where you might need to adjust your approach.

9. Self-Questionnaire

Instructions: Periodically, run through questions like, "Am I making choices based on fear or growth?" or "Are my decisions reactive or proactive?".

What it does for you: Encourages introspection about the driving forces behind your choices.

10. Goal Alignment Check

Instructions: Compare your choices to your short-term and long-term goals. Do they move you closer to or further from these goals?

What it does for you: Keeps you on track with your objectives, ensuring your decisions propel you towards your desired future.

Remember, every choice, big or small, steers the direction of your life. By regularly assessing the way you make decisions, you empower yourself to build a life that truly resonates with who you are and who you aspire to be.

CHAPTER SIX

The Power of Personal Responsibility in Spiritual Growth IT STARTS WITH YOU

ANALYSIS OF HOW ACCOUNTABILITY ACCELERATES SPIRITUAL MATURITY AND DEEPENS THE CONNECTION WITH THE DIVINE

You've embarked on a remarkable journey, one that intertwines the human and the Divine, the earthly and the spiritual. At the heart of this journey, nestled deep within its intricate layers, lies a powerful principle: personal responsibility. It's the understanding that the path to spiritual maturity starts with you. By embracing this notion, you can accelerate your spiritual growth and forge a deeper, more intimate connection with the Divine.

Imagine a gardener tending to their garden. Each seed planted, each weed removed, each decision made, impacts the garden's health and vitality. Similarly, in the landscape of your spiritual life, every choice you make, every action you undertake, carries significance. By taking responsibility for these choices, by acknowledging that it starts with you, you nurture your spiritual garden, allowing it to flourish and thrive.

Personal responsibility empowers you. No longer are you swayed by the winds of external influences, but you stand firm, rooted in the understanding of your role in your spiritual evolution. Recognizing that you are the architect of your spiritual destiny is liberating. It frees you from the chains of passivity and propels you towards proactive spiritual endeavors.

Now, consider the times you've faced challenges or obstacles in your spiritual journey. By adopting a mindset of personal responsibility, you can view these challenges not as hindrances but as opportunities for growth. It's a shift in perspective, one that transforms stumbling blocks into stepping stones. When you take charge, when you understand that it starts with you, you become adept at navigating these challenges, using them as catalysts for spiritual evolution.

But what about your connection with the Divine? How does personal responsibility deepen this bond? By taking responsibility for your actions, thoughts, and emotions, you align yourself with the Divine's will. In many religious and spiritual traditions, adherents are encouraged to seek the Divine's guidance and align their will with that of the higher power. By acknowledging your role in this relationship, by realizing that it starts with you, you actively participate in this divine dance, drawing closer to the source of all creation.

Furthermore, personal responsibility cultivates a sense of gratitude. When you take charge of your spiritual journey, you begin to recognize the countless blessings and opportunities that come your way. This gratitude, in turn, enhances your connection with the Divine, fostering a relationship built on love, appreciation, and mutual respect.

In conclusion, as you traverse the path of spiritual growth, always remember the power of personal responsibility. Recognize that it starts with you. Embrace this principle, let it guide your steps, and watch as it transforms your spiritual journey, deepening your connection with the Divine and accelerating your ascent towards spiritual maturity.

***

CHAPTER SEVEN

Breaking Free from the Blame Game: Practical Steps

A GUIDE TO HELP READERS MOVE FROM A MINDSET OF BLAME TO ONE

OF RESPONSIBILITY, OFFERING ACTIONABLE STEPS AND EXERCISES.

Life often throws curveballs, doesn't it? Sometimes you're left reeling, wondering why things happened the way they did. It's tempting, and all too easy, to shift the blame to someone else, to external circumstances, or even to fate. But what if, instead of playing the blame game, you chose a different path? One where you took charge, embraced responsibility, and sought growth. Ready to start? Here's a guide designed just for you, to help shift from blame to accountability.

1. Introspection is Key

Before you can change, you need to understand yourself. Dedicate some quiet time daily, even if it's just a few minutes. Reflect on your actions, decisions, and reactions. What patterns emerge? When do you tend to lay blame, and why? Understand that this isn't a session for self-critique but rather for self-awareness.

2. Challenge Your Thoughts

The next time you find yourself blaming someone or something, pause. Ask yourself: "Is this truly the cause, or is there a part I played in this?" This act of questioning helps you see situations from a broader perspective and identifies areas where you can take responsibility.

3. Journaling

Start a responsibility journal. Every evening, jot down instances where you took responsibility and times when you slipped into the blame mindset. Over time, you'll notice patterns, and the very act of writing will make you more mindful of your choices.

4. Seek Feedback

Often, others can see what we might be blind to. Confide in a trusted friend or mentor. Ask them for honest feedback on when they see you taking responsibility and when they see you defaulting to blame. Their insights can be illuminating.

5. Empathy and Understanding

When situations go awry, instead of casting blame, try to understand the other person's perspective. Maybe they had a reason for their actions. This doesn't mean absolving them of responsibility but understanding the larger picture.

6. Practice Affirmations

Affirmations can rewire your brain and shift your mindset. Daily, repeat phrases like: "I am in charge of my actions," "I choose responsibility over blame," or "I grow when I acknowledge my role." Over time, these words will become your reality.

7. Seek Opportunities for Growth

Mistakes and challenges are inevitable. Instead of dwelling on the 'why me', shift to 'what can I learn'. By viewing challenges as opportunities, you transform them into stepping stones for personal and spiritual growth.

8. Celebrate Small Wins

Taking responsibility is a journey, not a destination. Celebrate the small victories along the way. Did you acknowledge a mistake and rectify it? Did you resist the urge to blame and instead sought understanding? These are milestones worth celebrating.

9. Surround Yourself with Role Models

Find individuals, be they historical figures, leaders, or friends, who exemplify personal responsibility. Their stories and actions can inspire and guide you in your journey.

10. Stay Humble

Remember, this journey is not about perfection but growth. There will be times you falter; it's human. The key is to recognize, learn, and continue moving forward.

In essence, breaking free from the blame game and embracing personal responsibility is transformative. Not only will it impact your spiritual growth, but it will also ripple out, positively influencing all areas of your life. So, as you turn the page on blame and start this new chapter of accountability, remember: every step you take brings you closer to the best version of yourself.

CHAPTER EIGHT

Stories from Scripture: Lessons on Accountability

DELVING INTO VARIOUS RELIGIOUS TEXTS TO EXTRACT LESSONS ON PERSONAL RESPONSIBILITY AND THE PITFALLS OF BLAME.

Throughout the ages, sacred texts have served as a compass, guiding humanity on its path. These scriptures, while ancient, still echo with timeless truths that resonate even today. Let's dive deep into some of these religious stories to unearth lessons on personal responsibility and the pitfalls of blame.

1. Adam and Eve (Genesis 3):

The first humans, according to the Bible, teach us about the repercussions of shifting blame. When confronted by God after eating the forbidden fruit, Adam blamed Eve, and Eve blamed the serpent. This shirking of responsibility led to consequences for all. The lesson? Taking ownership of our actions, rather than pointing fingers, is pivotal in our relationship with the Divine and with each other.

2. King David and Bathsheba (2 Samuel 11-12):
David, despite being a man after God's own heart, faltered. He sinned with Bathsheba and tried to cover it up. When the prophet Nathan confronted him with a parable, David immediately realized his wrongdoing and repented. His journey underscores the importance of recognizing our misdeeds, feeling genuine remorse, and striving to make amends.

3. Jonah and the Whale (Book of Jonah):
Jonah tried to run from a divine task, resulting in turmoil not just for him but for those around him. When he acknowledged his responsibility, he was released from the belly of the whale. Jonah's story is a profound reminder that avoiding our duties and responsibilities can lead to chaos, but owning up to them can bring redemption.

4. The Prodigal Son (Luke 15:11-32):
A young man squandered his inheritance and lived recklessly. Yet, when he hit rock bottom, he took responsibility for his actions and decided to return home and seek forgiveness. His father welcomed him back with open arms. The narrative illuminates the power of acknowledgment, repentance, and the endless capacity for forgiveness.

5. Job's Trials (Book of Job):
While Job was a righteous man, his life was filled with suffering. Throughout his trials, friends and even his wife suggested he must have sinned to deserve such punishment. Instead of blaming God or others, Job sought understanding and remained steadfast in his faith.

His story exemplifies the idea that blame is not always warranted, and hardships can sometimes exist independent of one's deeds.

6. Achan's Sin (Joshua 7):

After the fall of Jericho, Achan took some of the spoils for himself, against God's command. When the Israelites suffered defeat in their next battle, Joshua sought the Lord's counsel. Achan was eventually identified and confessed. The lesson here is twofold: the consequences of one's actions can affect the collective, and hidden sins, when brought to light, require acknowledgment and restitution.

These tales, culled from the annals of religious texts, are not mere stories. They are mirrors reflecting the human condition, challenges, and the potential for growth. Each narrative is a testament to the age-old struggle between blame and responsibility, between avoidance and acknowledgment. As you reflect upon these stories, let them serve as reminders and guideposts on your journey towards spiritual accountability.

CHAPTER NINE

The Freedom in Owning Your Journey

EXPLORATION OF THE LIBERATING FEELING THAT COMES WITH ACKNOWLEDGING ONE'S ACTIONS AND THEIR CONSEQUENCES.

Have you ever felt the weight of carrying unspoken truths, or the burden of blaming others for the trajectory of your life? Imagine, for a moment, setting down those burdens, feeling the lightness that floods in when you take control, own your decisions, and fully embrace your life's narrative. This chapter is an invitation for you to experience the profound liberation that accompanies such an act.

You might wonder, "What freedom? I've made mistakes, and taking ownership means facing them!" Indeed, it does. But here's the beauty: when you face those decisions head-on, they lose their power over you. By acknowledging them, you're not giving them a louder voice; you're silencing the haunting whispers that play in the background of your mind.

Have you ever noticed how the stories you tell yourself – the narratives of blame, the 'what ifs', the regrets – have a way of trapping you? They build walls, confining you to a past that's unchangeable. But when you shift your perspective, when you stand tall and say, "Yes, this happened. I made this choice. And here's how I will move forward," you're dismantling those walls brick by brick.

The world begins to open up in unexpected ways. When you stop looking outward to assign blame and start looking inward for growth and understanding, you unlock a vast landscape of potential. Remember, you're not just a product of your past; you're a creator of your future. By owning every step, stumble, victory, and lesson, you are carving out a path that's uniquely yours.

Moreover, there's an authenticity that emerges when you own your journey. People can sense it. They're drawn to the raw, real energy of someone who's unapologetically themselves. Relationships deepen, trust strengthens, and meaningful connections form when you step into your truth.

And perhaps, the most transformative aspect? Your relationship with yourself. The internal battles quieten. The tug-of-war between blame and responsibility eases. A newfound respect blossoms – for your resilience, your growth, and your journey.

So, as you move forward, remember this: Owning your journey isn't about never making mistakes or having regrets. It's about understanding that every twist, turn, and detour has shaped you. Embrace it, learn from it, and find the freedom that comes with saying, "This is my story, and I am its author."

***

Assessment Tools:

1. Personal Milestone Timeline

Instructions: Draw a timeline of your life and plot significant milestones, decisions, and events. Reflect on the lessons learned at each point.

What it does for you: Provides a visual representation of your journey and how each choice influenced your path.

2. Life Script Analysis

Instructions: List out the key beliefs, norms, or scripts you feel you've been conditioned to follow. Assess which ones serve you and which ones don't.

What it does for you: Helps you identify and rewrite limiting beliefs that might be dictating your journey.

3. Empowerment Scale

Instructions: On a scale of 1-10, regularly rate how in control you feel over your life's direction. Dive deeper into any recurring low points.

What it does for you: Provides a measurable way to track your sense of autonomy over time.

4. Goal Achievement Tracker

Instructions: List out short-term and long-term goals. Track your progress and the steps you're taking to achieve them.

What it does for you: Gives a clear view of how you're actively shaping your journey.

5. "What If" Journaling

Instructions: Write down scenarios where you gave away your power or followed someone else's path. Reflect on what would have happened if you had taken ownership.

What it does for you: Encourages you to see the potential in fully owning every decision and its outcomes.

6. Core Value Alignment

Instructions: List your core values and assess recent decisions or actions against them. Do they align?

What it does for you: Reinforces the importance of making choices that resonate with your deepest beliefs.

7. Feedback Circles

Instructions: Gather a group of trusted peers. Share personal stories or decisions and get feedback on how they perceive your ownership of your journey.

What it does for you: Offers external validation or insight into how well you're owning your path.

8. Visualization Exercises

Instructions: Regularly take time to visualize your ideal life. Compare it to your current trajectory.

What it does for you: Helps ensure that the journey you're owning aligns with your aspirations.

9. Past Reflection, Future Projection

Instructions: Reflect on where you were 5 years ago versus where you are now. Then, project where you'd like to be in another 5 years.

What it does for you: Encourages gratitude for growth and helps set intentional goals for the future.

10. Intuition Check-ins

Instructions: Periodically, take moments of stillness to check in with your intuition. Ask yourself if the path you're on feels right.

What it does for you: Promotes a deep connection with your inner compass and ensures your journey remains genuine to you.

Owning your journey is about recognizing the autonomy you have over your life's path. These tools aim to remind you of that power, ensuring that the path you tread is truly your own, full of purpose, growth, and self-determined direction.

CHAPTER TEN

The Transformative Power of Self-Realization

DESCRIBING THE METAMORPHOSIS THAT OCCURS WHEN ONE STOPS BLAMING EXTERNAL FACTORS AND STARTS LOOKING INWARD.

Have you ever stood at the edge of a clear, still pond and thrown in a stone? You've likely watched as the ripples spread out, affecting every part of the water. Similarly, the moment of self-realization, that instant when you truly see yourself and your role in your life's narrative, creates ripples that touch every aspect of your being. This chapter delves into the metamorphosis that occurs when you shift from pointing fingers at the world to turning an introspective gaze upon yourself.

First, let's clarify: what exactly is self-realization? It's that enlightening moment when you recognize and accept your true self – flaws, strengths, regrets, and all. It's when you understand that your reactions, decisions, and emotions stem not from external events but from your internal beliefs, narratives, and choices.

Now, picture this: as you start taking this inward journey, you might initially feel discomfort. After all, it's far easier to blame life's storms on external factors. But imagine the liberation of understanding that while you can't always control the world around you, you absolutely can control how you perceive and respond to it. This understanding, this self-realization, is akin to being handed the reins to your life's chariot.

Your relationships begin to change. As you peel back the layers of blame and unveil the core of your authentic self, your interactions take on a depth and authenticity previously unknown. Why? Because when you truly see yourself, you begin to see others in their entirety too. That coworker you once blamed for office tensions? You might now perceive their struggles and realize the role you played in the dynamic.

Your goals and dreams might shift too. As you become more aligned with your true self, you might discover aspirations and passions buried under years of societal expectations and self-imposed limitations. It's as if a veil lifts, revealing a horizon filled with possibilities tailored just for you.

Moreover, the peace and contentment that you've perhaps sought in external validations or material acquisitions start blossoming from within. You begin to understand that true happiness isn't about waiting for the storm to pass but learning to dance in the rain. It's about finding balance, even when the ground beneath feels shaky.

In essence, the transformative power of self-realization is profound. It's not merely about understanding who you are but also about recognizing the potential of who you can become. It's about realizing that the key to your happiness, growth, and fulfillment has been in your hands all along. So, as you forge ahead, remember: the journey inward might be the most significant expedition you ever undertake. Embrace it, for it promises landscapes more breathtaking than any you've ever seen.

Assessment Tools:

1. Self-Realization Journal

Instructions: Dedicate a journal to track moments of self-discovery, personal revelations, and significant realizations.

What it does for you: Provides a chronological record of your journey to self-awareness and the transformations you undergo.

2. Core Belief Examination

Instructions: List your core beliefs and challenge each one. Are they truly yours, or are they adopted from someone else?

What it does for you: Helps distinguish between external influences and genuine self-awareness.

3. Personal SWOT Analysis

Instructions: Identify your Strengths, Weaknesses, Opportunities, and Threats. Regularly update this as you grow.

What it does for you: A tool used often in business, but when applied personally, it gives clarity on internal and external factors affecting your journey.

4. Reflection Meditation

Instructions: Spend time in quiet reflection, focusing on understanding yourself without judgment.

What it does for you: Encourages deep introspection and increases moments of self-realization.

5. Feedback Gathering

Instructions: Ask trusted individuals for honest feedback about your character, strengths, and areas of growth.

What it does for you: Provides an external perspective, which can lead to deeper self-awareness when juxtaposed with your self-view.

6. "Who Am I?" Exercises

Instructions: Regularly ask yourself, "Who am I?" and list out attributes, beliefs, desires, and fears. Reflect on the evolving answers.

What it does for you: Allows for the tracking of personal evolution and realization over time.

7. Role Analysis

Instructions: Identify the various roles you play in life (e.g., parent, employee, friend). Assess how each aligns or conflicts with your authentic self.

What it does for you: Aids in understanding how external expectations might shape your perceptions and actions.

8. Vision Boarding

Instructions: Create a visual representation of your aspirations, desires, and self-concept.

What it does for you: Transforms abstract ideas of self into tangible visions, furthering self-understanding.

9. Habit Tracker with Intention

Instructions: Monitor daily habits but also jot down the 'why' behind them. Reflect on which habits align with your genuine self.

What it does for you: Clarifies which routines reinforce your true self and which might be products of external pressures or outdated beliefs.

10. Personal Growth Retreats

Instructions: Dedicate time, whether it's a day or a weekend, for deep introspection without daily distractions.

What it does for you: Immerses you in self-reflection, often leading to profound realizations about self.

Harnessing the transformative power of self-realization is pivotal to living authentically. Through these tools, you'll be better equipped to understand yourself, leading to personal transformations that resonate deeply with your true essence.

CHAPTER ELEVEN

The Transformative Power of Self-Realization (SPLIT)

Assessment Tools:

1. Self-Realization Journal

Instructions: Dedicate a journal to track moments of self-discovery, personal revelations, and significant realizations.

What it does for you: Provides a chronological record of your journey to self-awareness and the transformations you undergo.

2. Core Belief Examination

Instructions: List your core beliefs and challenge each one. Are they truly yours, or are they adopted from someone else?

What it does for you: Helps distinguish between external influences and genuine self-awareness.

3. Personal SWOT Analysis

Instructions: Identify your Strengths, Weaknesses, Opportunities, and Threats. Regularly update this as you grow.

What it does for you: A tool used often in business, but when applied personally, it gives clarity on internal and external factors affecting your journey.

4. Reflection Meditation

Instructions: Spend time in quiet reflection, focusing on understanding yourself without judgment.

What it does for you: Encourages deep introspection and increases moments of self-realization.

5. Feedback Gathering

Instructions: Ask trusted individuals for honest feedback about your character, strengths, and areas of growth.

What it does for you: Provides an external perspective, which can lead to deeper self-awareness when juxtaposed with your self-view.

6. "Who Am I?" Exercises

Instructions: Regularly ask yourself, "Who am I?" and list out attributes, beliefs, desires, and fears. Reflect on the evolving answers.

What it does for you: Allows for the tracking of personal evolution and realization over time.

7. Role Analysis

Instructions: Identify the various roles you play in life (e.g., parent, employee, friend). Assess how each aligns or conflicts with your authentic self.

What it does for you: Aids in understanding how external expectations might shape your perceptions and actions.

8. Vision Boarding

Instructions: Create a visual representation of your aspirations, desires, and self-concept.

What it does for you: Transforms abstract ideas of self into tangible visions, furthering self-understanding.

9. Habit Tracker with Intention

Instructions: Monitor daily habits but also jot down the 'why' behind them. Reflect on which habits align with your genuine self.

What it does for you: Clarifies which routines reinforce your true self and which might be products of external pressures or outdated beliefs.

10. Personal Growth Retreats

Instructions: Dedicate time, whether it's a day or a weekend, for deep introspection without daily distractions.

What it does for you: Immerses you in self-reflection, often leading to profound realizations about self.

Harnessing the transformative power of self-realization is pivotal to living authentically. Through these tools, you'll be better equipped to understand yourself, leading to personal transformations that resonate deeply with your true essence.

CHAPTER TWELVE

Conclusion

: CHARTING A NEW PATH FORWARD

Praise Break

In the midst of life's hustle and bustle, it's easy to get caught up in the grandiose goals, the major milestones, and the monumental changes that we yearn for. Yet, often overlooked are the small, incremental victories that pave the way to these grand moments. Just like how a house is built brick by brick, our successes, both big and small, are constructed by countless little achievements. Taking a 'Praise Break' is about recognizing and celebrating these small wins that contribute to the bigger picture of our journey.

Why Celebrate Small Wins?

1. **Momentum Builder:** Small wins can give you the momentum needed to push forward. Just like a snowball rolling down a hill, what starts small gathers speed and size as it goes

along.

2. **Boosts Confidence:** Every time you recognize and celebrate a small achievement, you reinforce the belief that you can, and will, succeed.

3. **Enhances Motivation:** By acknowledging the progress you're making, you're more likely to stay motivated in working towards your bigger goals.

4. **Fosters Gratitude:** Celebrating the small things helps foster an attitude of gratitude, which has been linked to increased happiness and well-being.

5. **Highlights Progress:** It's a reminder that you are moving forward, even if it's just one step at a time.

How to Take a Praise Break:

1. **Mindfulness and Reflection:** Start by being present in the moment. Take a few minutes each day to reflect on what you've accomplished, no matter how minor it might seem.

2. **Journaling:** Keep a 'Small Wins Journal'. Every day, jot down at least one thing that you consider a victory. Over time, flipping through this journal can offer immense encouragement.

3. **Share with Someone:** Talk to a friend or family member about your win. Their enthusiasm and pride can amplify your own feelings of accomplishment.

4. **Treat Yourself:** It could be something as simple as taking a longer break, having your favorite snack, or dedicating some time to a hobby you love.

5. **Physical Celebration:** Do a little dance, clap your hands, or simply take a deep, satisfying breath. A physical manifestation of your celebration can help in internalizing that joy.

6. **Affirmations:** Speak positivity into your life. Say something like, "I am proud of myself for..." or "I am making progress, one step at a time."

7. **Visualization:** Close your eyes and visualize the bigger goal. See this small win as a stepping stone leading you closer to that grand vision.

Celebrating the small wins doesn't mean losing sight of the bigger picture. Instead, it's a recognition that every big goal is made up of numerous smaller steps, each deserving of celebration. By incorporating 'Praise Breaks' into your routine, you not only honor your progress but also rejuvenate your spirit, preparing it for the next phase of the journey. So, the next time you achieve something, no matter how small, pause, acknowledge, and celebrate. Every step forward is a win, and every win is worth celebrating.

***

Now back to your regular reading of the conclusion:
As you've embarked on this journey of introspection and self-discovery, it's paramount to visualize and chart your way forward. This

chapter isn't just a conclusion but a beginning - the start of a life where you're the captain, steering with intention and clarity.

Your Spiritual Growth Chart:

(Imagine a chart divided into four main quadrants)

1. **Self-awareness:**

   - **Where you were:** Operating from blame, reacting rather than responding.

   - **Where you're heading:** Conscious awareness of emotions and actions, understanding the roots of reactions.

2. **Responsibility:**

   - **Where you were:** Externalizing fault, avoiding personal accountability.

   - **Where you're heading:** Embracing ownership of decisions, accepting outcomes, and learning from experiences.

3. **Growth & Learning:**

   - **Where you were:** Stagnation, repeating old patterns, and resisting change.

   - **Where you're heading:** Seeking knowledge, embracing change, and welcoming new challenges as opportunities for growth.

4. **Connection & Relationship:**

   - **Where you were:** Surface-level interactions, blaming others, building walls.

- ○ **Where you're heading:** Deep, meaningful relationships based on understanding, empathy, and genuine connection.

Now, imagine this chart as a living document, one that evolves as you do. Ponder upon where you fit now and where you'd like to be in each quadrant.

The path ahead won't always be smooth. At times, the allure of old patterns might beckon. But remember this: you've been handed a compass with this newfound knowledge. Every time you feel lost, pause, refer to your chart, and recalibrate.

With this new vision, you stand at a crossroads. Behind you is a road paved with blame, unfulfilled potential, and external influences. Ahead lies a path shimmering with possibility, self-awareness, and profound connection to both self and the Divine.

No journey is without its bumps and bends. But in taking ownership, seeking growth, and forging deep, authentic connections, you're not just walking a path; you're trailblazing. And this trail? It's not etched in blame or regrets but illuminated with lessons, love, and self-realization.

As you step forward, know that every moment is an opportunity. Every challenge, a lesson. Every interaction, a mirror. You possess all you need within you to chart this radiant path. So, with heart full and eyes clear, stride forth. Your journey, unburdened by blame and radiant with purpose, awaits.

Throughout this exploration, you've ventured deep into the heart of accountability, peeling back the layers of blame, unraveling the tales of external adversaries, and discovering the profound power that resides within you. The central revelation is simple, yet transformative:

The real battleground is not outside, but within the confines of one's mind and heart.

Blaming the adversary has been a safety net, a shield to hide behind when confronted with uncomfortable truths. But every time you pointed a finger outward, three pointed back at you. This journey illuminated those hidden fingers, revealing the personal choices, habits, and narratives that shaped your experiences.

You've learned that true empowerment stems from acknowledging one's role in life's dance. To say, "It's me, not an external force," is to reclaim a sense of agency. It's an invitation to introspect, to grow, and to evolve. To step out of the shadows of blame and into the light of self-awareness.

But this conclusion is not an end. It's a new beginning. A call to continually reflect, learn, and transform. As you move forward, may you carry with you the wisdom that while external forces exist, your reaction and response to them define your journey. The adversary might be a concept, a force, or a presence, but it's your choices, words, and actions that shape your spiritual path.

In the narrative of your life, you are the protagonist, the author, and the reader. The adversities and challenges are but plot twists, urging you to grow, adapt, and rise. As you pen the next chapters, let them be filled with stories of strength, resilience, and evolution, rather than blame.

So, as you close this book and re-enter the world, remember this: The power to shape your destiny has always been within you. It's not about the adversary; it's about you. Embrace this truth, and watch as your journey transforms from one of blame to one of profound personal growth and spiritual enlightenment.

CHAPTER THIRTEEN

Transitioning from Blaming the Adversary to Taking Personal Responsibility

1. Self-Reflection Journaling:

Instructions: Dedicate a few minutes each evening to jot down moments where you felt the urge to blame external factors. Ask yourself why and try to trace back to the root cause.

What it does for you: By doing this regularly, you'll soon notice patterns in your behavior and begin to recognize the triggers that prompt you to externalize blame.

2. Blame vs. Accountability Chart

Instructions: Draw a two-column chart. Whenever you catch yourself placing blame (on the adversary or anything external), write it in the 'Blame' column. Next, rewrite the situation in the 'Accountability' column, framing it from a perspective of personal responsibility.

What it does for you: This visual tool helps you rewire your thought patterns, moving you from a mindset of blame to one of empowerment.

3. Daily Affirmation Reminders

Instructions: Start your day with affirmations that emphasize personal power and responsibility, such as "I am in control of my reactions," or "I choose how I respond to challenges." Repeat them whenever you feel the urge to *blame. What it does for you:* Over time, these affirmations act as a mental shield, deflecting the instinct to blame and reinforcing personal agency.

4. Mindfulness and Meditation

Instructions: Dedicate a few minutes daily to sit quietly, focusing on your breath and being present. If a blaming thought arises, observe it without judgment, then gently return to your breath.

What it does for you: This practice heightens self-awareness, making it easier to catch and rectify moments of blame in real-time.

5. Feedback Circle

Instructions: Form a trusted circle of friends or family. Grant them permission to point out moments when you might be shirking responsibility. Be open to their observations.

What it does for you: Sometimes, an external perspective can shed light on blind spots you might miss.

6. The "5 Whys" Techniques

Instructions: Whenever a situation arises where blame feels imminent, ask yourself "Why?" Dig deep into the reason behind your feelings. Often, by the time you ask the fifth "Why?", you'll reach the underlying issue.

What it does for you: This method helps in getting to the root cause of the problem, highlighting areas where you can take control.

7. Visual Imagery Exercise

Instructions: Close your eyes and visualize two paths. One is murky, filled with shadows (the blame path). The other is lit brightly, clear, and inviting (the accountability path). Every time you face a challenge, imagine yourself choosing the brighter path.

What it does for you: Visualization reinforces positive behavior, encouraging you to make better choices.

As you utilize these tools, remember, it's not about perfection but progress. There will be days when old habits resurface, but with commitment and the right tools, you'll find yourself transitioning from a world of blame to one where you're in the driver's seat, navigating with confidence and clarity.